Advance Praise for
Toxic Masculinity

A young boy first discovers firearms by the side of his abuelito, sees violence first hand in a childhood home while dreaming closets to be portals only to apologize as an adult. As a young man he is caged alongside more young men, just like him, contemplating their own guilt. An abuelita in a crowded home of extended family prepares dinner to the specification of his conspiracy obsessed tio. As a grown man now, he, he sits in traffic, watching his fellow motorists attempt to capture selfies with a possible freeway suicide.

Fernando Albert Salinas's collection *Toxic Masculinity* is a rough book. These are poems that pull no punches. In the case of Salinas the phrase "brutal honesty" falls woefully short. Despite these scenes of cruelty, apathy and the pain we inflict upon each other for reasons often unknown to ourselves. At the center of this incredible work there is no malice. There is only a refusal to lie. And in that refusal Salinas captures our real faces in all our faults, in all our rages and stupors and yes our deep desire to do better.

This collection is an unwavering mirror, challenging and painful as it may be.

— **Matt Sedillo**,
author of *Mowing Leaves of Grass*

Fernando Albert Salinas is a damn fine poet and a mensch, definitely a bro--feo, fuerte, y formal. What comes out in his poems is brazen and fearless and sometimes tough to read. Perhaps it's what makes him the incredible workshop teacher of students, of kids. Perhaps it's why I have to take a long walk after reading his work.

— **Ricardo Means Ybarra**,
Malibu, CA Poet Laureate

Toxic Masculinity is a poetic memoir with jagged edges that explores the transitive natures of masculinity, violence, and the prismatic ways they intersect. Fernando Salinas is a modern-day Chicano Virgil, guiding his reader through the nine circles of a Los Angeles barrio. His poems bear witness, bleed, throb like a bruise against the page, and examine the poisons we are taught to drink as boys & as men."

— **Brennan DeFrisco**,
author of *A Heart With No Scars*

TOXIC MASCULINITY:
The Misadventures of a Barrio Boy

FLOWERSONG
PRESS

poems by
Fernando Albert Salinas

FLOWERSONG
PRESS

FlowerSong Press
Copyright © 2021 by Fernando Albert Salinas
ISBN: 978-1-953447-82-1
Library of Congress Control Number: 2021947018

Published by FlowerSong Press
in the United States of America.
www.flowersongpress.com

Cover Art by Alexis Salinas
Cover Art Design by Alexis Salinas
Author Photo Credit: Anthony Angel Salinas
Set in Adobe Garamond Pro

No part of this book may be reproduced without written permission from the Publisher.

All inquiries and permission requests should be addressed to the Publisher.

For

Aunt Margaret Arzate
Margaret Cruz Arzate
Joe Arzate
Fernando Joe Salinas
Gavino Salinas Sr.
Sara Maldonado
Nanette Salinas
Alexis Salinas
Seth Salinas
Javan Salinas
Anthony Salinas
Michael Salinas
Erica Salinas

CONTENTS

xi   Preface

xii   Foreword

Part 1 - THE BOY

2   Lullaby for Panchita; after Federico Garcia Lorca, On Lullabies

4   El Rancho Grande

5   Directions

7   Macho, a la Brava

9   Watts

11   Borrowed Time

13   Asada

15   Sonia

16   Moscas

18   Broken Joystick

19   Physical Education

20   Coda

22   Grace

24 On My Way to See Colors

26 I'm Going to Miss You, Dumbass

28 Negro (Original Gangster)

29 The Last Time I See You

30 What You Won't Do For Love

31 Goodnight, Gorilla. Goodnight Gangster

32 A Tree Without Roots is Just Another Piece of Wood

36 Fodder

37 Shag Carpet

39 Conspiracy Theories

41 De Familia

42 Birth to Death

44 La Cocina

45 5 Fingers (Indica Leaf)

47 Swapping Sillies

49 Something She Was Going to Tell You

Part 2 - THE MAN

54 County Zoo

55 Blind Faith

57 Unnatural Remedies for Fairness

59 Wonder is Enough For Now

60 For Fathers Who Pay to Have Their Children Beaten

63 True Story

64 Bye, Dad...

65 This is My Body

67 Antibiotic Antidepressants

68 Some search for love between stained sheets, while others search for death as though it's hidden between the sheets of their shredded wrists

71 Finally Letting Go

72 She Spilled Out of Her Low Tide Blue Jeans

73 Dry Hump

74 Insomnia

75 1 Day in Perspective

77 Fluffy

79 Zombies Run 10ks

80 The Radical Pair Mechanism

81 Every Man's Fantasy; After Friday Gretchen, Every Woman's Fantasy

83 Far, But Not Gone

85 Escape Velocity

86 To Whom it May Concern

87 Watch Him Fall Forever

89 Zero Tolerance: Miseducation; After Federico Garcia Lorca, New York (Office and Denunciation)

92 Floating Echo

94 The Walking Dead

96 M249 Squad Automatic Weapon

97	Resilience
101	No!
104	Orange Man Versus the Universe
106	Let's Go

Acknowledgements

Thank you to all of the editors, presses, and publishers that have given my poetry a place to be read, seen, and/or heard:

#Immigration: "Zero Tolerance: Miseducation; After Federico García Lorca, New York (Office and Denunciation)"

2 Degrees, Translated by Luis Antonio Pichardo: "The Walking Dead"

Askew Poetry Journal: "El Rancho Grande", "Moscas", "Sonia" and "This is My Body"

Chaparral: "Watch Him Fall Forever"

City of Ventura, Art Tales Awards: "Blind Faith"

Confused Muse: "My Therapist"

Into the Teeth of the Wind: "Asada"

Lengua Larga, Boca Abierto: A Tree Without Roots is Just Another Piece of Wood and "Unnatural Remedies for Fairness"

Lummox Press: On My Way to See Colors

Maple Leaf Rag IV, Portals Press: "Borrowed Time"

Mexican Schools: "Physical Education"

Miramar: "Directions", "Let's Go" and "Macho, a la Brava"

Poetry Super Highway: "Dry Hump" and "She Spilled Out of Her Low Tide Blue Jeans"

Poetry Zone Anthology: "Broken Joystick"

Sage Trail: "Antibiotic Antidepressants" and "Insomnia"

Santa Barbara Voices: "1 Day in Perspective"

Scribblers: "De Familia"

Solo Novo: "Fodder"

Solo Novo Press's *Psalms of Cinder and Silt*: "Fluffy"

The Aviator, Editor's Choice Award: "To Whom it May Concern"

This is Not a Journal: "La Cocina"

Preface

This book is a requiem. The original title of this book was *The World Is a Barrio*. The idea was to pay homage to the band, WAR. The song, "The World Is a Ghetto" inspired me to see the world differently. It encouraged me to see the world beyond the one I lived in. And, the world I was raised in was one of gangs, sex, drugs, violence, poverty, systemic/structural racism, education inequity, health disparity, food insecurity, patriotism, and death. A ghetto. A barrio. For whatever reason, so many in the world want to forget this world existed and still does. Some cancel-culture cancels culture. I used the title for my second novel instead.

Then, I wanted to title the book, *The Pinche Piñata*. This title was a metaphor—a play on the expression, "Mi vida loca." It was the original title of my second novel. I shopped the manuscript back in 2011. No one was ready to publish a book that examined transgender identity development and gender dysphoria. No one wanted to watch a boy grow up in the barrio and survive his machismo family. Or, maybe it was because less than 10 percent of the fiction-authors published are people of color.

The meaning of the title, *The Pinche Piñata*, was intended to describe how my life felt. I have been a piñata. Life was the stick. That stick beat me again and again until I finally broke. And, that was when all the good stuff came pouring out—everyone ran up to take a piece. However, I felt uncomfortable cursing every time I told someone the title. It is not something I do very often. So, I called my daughter. She says, "Dad, your work is about the damage of being nurtured in an environment of toxic masculinity." She says, "How about, Toxic Masculinity?"

Another proud-dad moment. Of course . . . It was not life I survived, you survived, he survived, she survived, they survived, we survived. It was toxic masculinity. This book is a collection of poems based upon the lives of those that I have grieved, loved, feared, respected, and survived.

Foreword

I was surprised and honored to receive Fernando Albert Salinas' request that I write the foreword for this extraordinary collection of poems, *Toxic Masculinity: The Misadventures of a Barrio Boy*. I have known Fernando for several years through our work together with the non-profit California Poets in the Schools, an organization that yearly brings poetry composition workshops to almost 25,000 K-12 students throughout the state. He has been our enthusiastic area coordinator for Ventura County and Poet-Teacher as well. Two years, ago Fernando joined me and others on the Cal Poets board where he has taken on important outreach projects, acted as mentor to young poets, created beautiful artistic posters of poetry for public distribution and recently brought a new board member to us from Ventura. A consensus builder, Fernando is soft-spoken but not shy. I have been impressed with his humility and the quality of his listening. As illustrated in this collection, Fernando is fierce in his observance of detail and in his ability through powerful language to paint dazzling imagery. He has related to me that most of the voices of these poems are his own or of members of his family.

In contrast to Fernando, I am not from a big city. I grew up in a small town in the San Joaquin Valley with a significant Mexican American population though most of my exposure to Mexican culture at an early age came through hanging around the bracero camp where my father's company provided appetizing meals for the workers who came from Mexico to toil in the fields and orchards of my county. My parents were bilingual and our family would eat alongside them and the kitchen staff often. In contrast, Fernando's poems inhabit the urban streets and Chicano neighborhoods of Southern California. Their smoke is the exhaust of speeding cars, not the dust of country roads. Their spines and blooms are not the well-tended rose garden but the place "where lopped heads feed flowers/ buried in the barrio botanical garden" (*Resilience*). Their children are not the attendees at the migrant labor camp where I taught one summer but the kids that roam city streets with guns and gangs.of those that I have grieved, loved, feared, respected, and survived.

This is a book that in poem after poem reveals the ragged as well as incandescent intersections between Mexican, Chicano and Anglo residents and their ways of understanding and dealing with the world. I was eager to dive into this world, but I was not prepared for the stunning imagery, the inescapability from its truth and moments of utter surprise that I felt while reading *Toxic Masculinity: The Misadventures of a Barrio Boy*. Have you ever felt bound to a poem? That was the sensation I had as I read nearly every poem in this work. I came across images so insistent they seemed to dangle in front of me as if in still air, saying *Look at Me!*, as in *Unnatural Remedies for Fairness*: "Take milk powder,/ papaya and honey/ Smear this on his forehead before bed/ and by morning,/ he will be invisible to the police" and in *Macho, a la Brava*: "I waited for the tears to come, and then I realized that they were already there, only they had been caught by my blindfold."

This breathtaking collection of poetry is divided by time into two sections, *The Boy* and *The Man*. In the first section a sweet kind of tenderness ("My *abuelita* wrapped my bones in flour tortillas" in La *Cocina* and "I'll never forget how her blond hair/ glowed beneath the porch light" in *Grace*) faces the importance of rigid roles and violence as a part of daily life: "his fists are boulders/ wrapped in buffalo hide/ clenched like his teeth" and, as the grandpa tells a young immigrant, "you better listen here/ I am an American/ I fought for the land/ you snuck into" in *A Tree Without Roots Is Just Another Piece of Wood*. Regret and despair surround everyone in the barrio and the boy experiences an overwhelming confusion and at times, loneliness, trying to understand his surroundings at a young age, as in the poem *Physical Education*: "I can't remember my destination." There is a definite sense of place and time in these poems, as in "my grandma/ slamming the cabinets/ to make sure she wasn't/ the only one awake/ before sunrise." Salinas exquisitely portrays Chicano culture through strong family ties, its rich cuisine, its car culture and the importance of religion and hard work. The poet's striking alliteration with its juxtaposition of a teenager's risky behavior and the details of street cred is exemplified in "I juke zigzags into blind spots/ duck and dodge bullets/ past a pristine white '74 Monte Carlo" in *On My Way To See Colors.* There is the initiation into the street life, gangs and looking up to another kind of mentor: "he'd write letters in beautiful ink/ and remind me,/ 'Mijo, have a dream'" in *Negro (Original Gangster).* Salinas' language is integral to the tone of his startling poetry, as can be seen in *The Last Time I see You*: "the setting sun's/ sides are stabbed by silver clouds/An engine revs."

In *Birth To Death*, a significant poem about the grandmother's death, I came across the striking lines "I remember the time you took scissors/ to my calla lilies/ I was furious/ You said, *It's because -/ every once in a while,/ we have to start over."* I was reminded of Diego Rivera's glorious paintings *Girl with Lilies* (1941) and *The Flower Vendor* (1942) and of the other images of calla lilies that Rivera painted. Rivera employed them as an ode to the fertility and suffering of native and mestizo peoples. In Mexico calla lilies are important symbols of purity, funerals and death. They are a quintessential example of Mexican flora and known by various names such as *lirio, alcatraz, azucena* and *cala*, depending on the state. Indeed, it is poignant to come upon these emblematic lilies in a poem about the grandmother's death.

In the section titled *The Man,* the boy is no longer just the witness to events. He lives the hurt, pain and self-doubt more intensely in his search for belonging and even redemption. There is a restless energy and dread in these poems as in "our skin turns gray as the floor, walls, bars, justice" in *County Zoo* and "knowing now is not the time to tell you/ we are always touching the sky" in *Wonder Is Enough For Now.* We are reminded that this poet lives in the barrio: "A siren's whine wanes/outside our window/ A cool breeze sighs/ with the city's raspy hiss/ through the dusty screen" in *Far But Not Gone.* Here it is as if the dusty screen interacts with the raspy hiss, at the same time muffling and intensifying the emotion. One feels the night in many of these poems, as in "The nicotine-stained fingernail moon/ scratched dark cold reason" in *To Whom It May Concern.*

There is no lack of anger, rebellion and distrust, beauty, machismo, barrio slang and the fight between dystopia and *cariño* in this second section. Salinas' imagery continues to be fresh and striking throughout: "The endless bleaching of color/ and the purging of hope, shackled/ by pale patriotics" and "I spit tears in your faces" in *Zero Tolerance: Miseducation*. Resistance lives with despair in this poem: "I am only a desperate whisper/ What more can I do than ask the ICE to melt/ one warm breath at a time?"

To my view the most riveting poem in the second section is *Unnatural Remedies for Fairness* because of the way it reveals the burden of continuing prejudice and racial inequality. It hurts so deeply because it speaks of the agonizing Mexican grandmother who cannot accept the skin color of her own grandson. She offers a list of folk remedies recommended to lighten it:

> "She would not hold my son.
> As though his café skin,
> richer than a dark roast Grande drip
> was a plague that could be passed
> through touch.
> Pobre Morenito, she cried"
>
> .....
>
> "Rub his arms with a skinned potato repeatedly
> and no one will assume he speaks something
> other than English."
>
> .....
>
> "Mix baking soda with water
> and let it sit for 15 minutes.
> Use it to bleach away his darkness and
> no one will ever call him a...
> Nevermind.
> Such words will never be said in this house."

Toxic Masculinity will make you pause and make you think because it demands to be seated at the table and reckoned with. Its searing poetry will be read widely and appreciated. In college I studied Latin American literature and, as a poet myself, I can say that this enlightening book is consequential. It will take its place among the important works in both American and Latin American literature.

— **Nels Goñi Christianson**
Santa Monica, California

THE BARRIO BOY

Lullaby for Panchita; after Federico García Lorca, On Lullabies

No llores, Panchita.
Don't you cry.
The man at the door will stop knocking.
Sooth the crumb cast by God
when left in your womb
to rot in this world with you.
Appreciate how it screams louder
than the man in your bed snores.
He too dreams of anywhere but here.

Cálmate, Panchita.
Calm yourself.
The man at the door will stop knocking.
Before morning, his child will hush and
you will forget it exists again.
But first, see him yearn
for some worthless thing
framed by the window
between the barren cabinets.

Tranquila, Panchita.
Quiet down.
The man at the door
spends hours picturing your face
shimmer upon the dirty lake
you wish to drown yourself in.
When the man in your bed
leaves to pluck devil's fruit,
the man at the door
will return to place his strawberry
upon your dry lips and refresh you.

Pobrecita, Panchita.
Tomorrow, the man at the door
will enter to rip apart
the tangles of your thoughts
and devour you with starving fingers.
Remember to wipe him from
your thighs. Remember to pray
to the one who has forgotten
you. Ask Him to help you forget
the man who comes to the door.

El Rancho Grande

I am so unfamiliar
with the metal which appears
at my abuelito's hip, that
at first I do not realize it is a gun.
I drape over his sun-browned forearm
muscles twist and harden across my chest.
He does not move.
He holds his aim.
You have to shoot coyotes in the head.
Otherwise, when they die,
rattlesnakes will crawl from their stomachs.
I follow the barrel of his gun
into the field and instead of a reptile or animal
there is a man, frozen mid-step,
shirtless.
Dirty bare feet under sun-bleached jeans
trespassing,
ridiculously white teeth
exposed by thin wide-spread lips.
The man is smiling.
You see—he's lazy.
He harvests others' work.
He's not ashamed to steal.
My abuelito lifts me by my armpit and
places me on his back and then,
he fires.

Directions

Descend through opaque smog and
explode into an aerial view of Los Angeles.
Dodge skyscrapers and swerve between
parked cars heading south on the 405.
Exit Century Blvd. and stop for a red light.
A transient will drool over his bloated tongue,
black gums, and spit between the gap
of his front teeth into a soiled tube sock,
wipe Your feet, and then Your eyes
until the world seems a little brighter.

The spit-shine-cleaner will stick out
the lighter side of his hand for change, but
the light will turn green. And,
with Your glorious ass to him,
he'll make two fists--
every jagged fingernail digging into the palms of his hands
except for his thumbs and middle fingers, and
he'll jab those, first, at the dirty brown sky,
then at You, but You won't see him.

Take a left. Then, another past
a man selling bundles of roses from an island,
gabachos in designer business suits trading
limp presidents for warm tamales
a boy selling oranges packed in pillowcase-size clear plastic bags,
past kids selling drugs from street corners, and
girls selling themselves from sidewalk curbs.

You won't see Your reflection in the liquor store window
cracked up in Ys, but You might find my placaso
on the old brick building where spray paint crosses out descendants
on the graffiti family tree of La Raza.

Ignore the homeless woman sitting with five children
under the age of four by the adult bookstore.
I need You. Rise back up off the street,
over the houses, watch for planes roaring by
beginning their descent into LAX.
Perch on the telephone pole tagged LNX.
I'll be in house there, in my room on my knees
searching for the toy my abuelita said
I'd never find until I asked You
to forgive me for not believing in You.

Macho, a la Brava

Hold on . . . 1, 2, 3, and by 18, 19, 20, . . .
hit it like a man, I thought I was going to be sick. And then, the piñata came at me so I swung hard, but instead of hitting it, it hit me, knocked the stick out of my hand, busted my lip, and made my chin throb with its own heartbeat from rope burn.

I felt around the grass and found the stick right as Porky Pig kicked me in the nuts. I swung wildly, angry, and seeking vengeance. I could hear the decorative streamers cutting through the black smoke blooming from the barbecue. I could smell my father's chicken burning.

Hey, loco, watcha! This bato is pissed now!

I went to peek under my blindfold and felt someone punch me in the back of my head.

No cheating! Can you believe this shit?

I swung with all I had and missed everything but the air. The stick flew out of my hand. The German Shepherd, Kingy, yapped. I tried to catch my breath and waited. I waited for the beating my father was going to give me. I waited for them to start calling me names. I waited for the tears to come, and then I realized that they were already there, only they had been caught by my blindfold.

Get up, lil' boxer. No crying on your birthday!

My tío took my arm and lifted me to my feet. His calloused fingertips poked between my forehead and the blue bandana blindfold, and he took it off me. He pulled a knife out of his back pocket that could easily have passed for a machete.

Fuck this pinche piñata, ese! You gonna make my nephew cry?

My tío jabbed the piñata in the eye and then the neck. He pierced it over and over again until candy and almonds spilled out of its guts, and I was laughing—laughing at how crazy he looked and laughing at how he had ripped off Porky's arm in the assault. I smeared snot from my nose and took the heavy knife he placed in my hand, plunging the blade into Porky until the yard was littered with colored paper. My family cheered as though they were witnessing me slaughter my first pig.

Watts

Her two kids, 7 and 4,
are in the backseat
of the Phoenix Red 1974 VW Beetle.
Her husband, passed out
in the passenger seat
with his safety belt on.
She's singing Angel Baby
along with Rosie and the radio
waiting for that red light on Imperial.

You can see the smile of her almond eyes
in the rear-view mirror. And, she is singing,
Oh, oh, I love you. Oh, oh, I do,
when the driver's side window explodes
and the shadow of an arm
reaches in to unlock the door.
The man holding a knife—
the one wearing a navy blue
satin baseball jacket, yanks
a worthless gold chain with the letters
MOM spelled in cursive off her neck,
then demands more.

The barely 5-foot woman shouts back,
"We're just like you! Broke!"
She isn't lying.
I remember watching her search for change
between the seats of the car
to find enough gas money to get us home.

I've never understood cruelty.
I still wonder

if that desperate man
punctured her lung
because he didn't believe her.
I still wonder why the police officer
stood where there was once a window,
yelling, telling her to get the car
out of the middle of the street
while she was bleeding out.
It may have been the first time
I saw my father cry.

Borrowed Time

Aztec warriors
in bandanas and Dodger blue
chanted mantras,
waved knives and guns
over tattooed tears,
told of time spent
beating a man until he lied
and denied he was witness to a recent homicide.
They boasted about how messed up they got before
hustling, slinging, robbing, stabbing,
shooting, breaking, taking
whatever they wanted, making one man yank the
                                          cord strung across the bus
because at the time
there were probably 12 of them
and only 4 of us
and he just wanted to get off
anywhere they weren't.

Brakes screeched first, and then
a boy dragged by his blonde hair.
He grabbed at anything he could
to keep from being pulled off onto
their street and into their city.
I heard a veterano say,
Nice watch, ese.
And, sure enough, that gabacho had time
wrapped around his wrist like he owned it.

Yeah, I heard the boy screaming
but when the bus jerked away
I wasn't about to jump into his grave,

so I tossed the first fistful
of dirt onto his coffin,
like anyone would
and turned away because
that watch, only worth about fifty,
was worth more than anything I'd ever owned
and maybe
it was just his time to go.

Asada

He should have known better,
but Alejandro made the mistake
of hobbling over to my tío Juan
and ratting out Cico for
giving him a Charlie horse in the leg.
And, to make matters worse,
he didn't say anything.
He just stood there
Wu-huh-hah-hu-uh-ing.
Tu sabes, hyperventilating
como un chango.

Why you crying? Is something broken?

No words. No intelligible response—

Mira, Consuela, I found La Llorona.

My cousin's pride drained from his eyes—
a little more respect lost with each tear shed.

Tío Juan reached for his thick leather belt, and asked,
You want me to give you a reason to cry?
And just like that, Alejandro found his courage.

My tío gripped Alejandro's wrist and told him to make a fist—
¡*Palo malo!* ¡*Palo malo!*
Ow! Ow!
Alejandro's head bounced away from his knuckles
each time he punched himself in the ear.

And to the whole family, Tío Juan shouted, laughing,

Look at him crying like a little girl! but then,
he placed his lips to Alejandro's ear, and whispered,
Now go play where I don't have to hear you cry.
And when he isn't looking, hit him back.
But, get him good. So he doesn't forget it!
Mira, and to make sure he learned, he slammed
Alejandro's fist into the side of his head again,
¡Palo malo!—
'cause it stings demasiado there,
¿Que no?

Sonia

By 5, I knew aliens mated with apes
And Ma(ya)nkind came into being.
By 9, I knew angels mated with humans
And made giants.
At 11, I watched you
Pump pedals
On my Huffy
Setting the standard
For every other woman
Whoever leaves me.
Only, you never came back
And your brother
Kept my bike.

Moscas

Cholitas with blue eye-shadow and
Aqua Net hairdos tore each other's clothes off
for everyone in the barrio to see. A nipple,
the size of the small tortillas my grandma made
with leftover flour, flopped out from under
a yellow tube-top.

The girl with the gold cross retaliated and two quarts
of café con leche spilled out of a black lace bra.
There were sharp smacking sounds like the ones
my grandma made working masa
for tamales Christmas Eve.

It was summer.
Tiny beads of sweat gathered on the dim mustache
of the girl with coarse hair on her arms.
Their perfumes covered the smell of garbage
collected in the sidewalk gutter. They bit
into smooth shoulders. Mascara smeared the others'
skin, brown lipstick onto each others' necks. A Vans
tennis shoe flipped off one of the girl's feet
as she stumbled back. She stayed on the ground
with her open hand out in front of her face
to keep the other girl away. One of her earrings
was torn out of her ear, and she panted, heaving for air.

I'd seen my mother lain in front of my father
on the floor in this same defense and then
I remembered what it felt like when I wanted to
melt into the ground rather than be hit again.
So, I reached out to help the girl up, but all she did
was cover her exposure with her forearm.

Someone from behind told me to stay out of it,
so I backed away and for a moment
I wished I had never seen her nakedness.

Broken Joystick

His hands,
they were so big then.

I thought raindrops taste like cotton candy
and mountains were dinosaurs
resting under dirty blankets,
I dreamed closets were
portals to other dimensions.
My ears stung, warm as
black leather left in Indian sun.
I thought pennies
tasted like blood
and that closing your eyes
could make you invisible.

We were so small,
back then.

When I thought my skin
would finally tear
under his heavy fists,
this coward let you take the blame
and you stared at me.
Your eyes scream, WHY?
Your voice screams, NO!

I am so, so sorry.

Physical Education

I hope it wasn't you standing beside me. I didn't look, but I could feel you there. The initiation was beyond torture, worse than the 8 laps, 100 jumping jacks, 50 push-ups and the ninety-ninth of one hundred sit-ups that made me let out a fart next to Lilia Torres. I could never look at her again. I'm sure I heard her laugh. It was traumatic—the shower freezing, hot tears steaming from my cheeks. The PE teacher shouting, Make sure you scrub your ass and pits. I was on a bus one day—I can't remember my destination, but everyone on it seemed content to be headed forward together. A man sitting behind me whispered guttural wisdom, We can never truly know what we look like. So, how could I begin to describe myself as a boy? Feeble, so thin, while the showerhead spit, I must have appeared to be trying to dodge its streams. The water cracking upon the cold, piss-yellow tile as loud as a child screaming for help. Do you remember the boy hiding in the bangs of his curly dripping hair, cupping his great insecurity? I will never be able to dress for you—to cover up. We have never been taught to un-see. I hope you still don't see me standing naked in the halls, by the lockers, at lunch, in the cafeteria eating a bologna sandwich, drinking naked juice, at the dance holding Ruby's hand, wishing she was her sister, at Church, and at the funeral of that kid that got shot in a drive by. It would be better if we could forget that day.

Coda

Plinking cans become incurious
Round shots stream within the smooth
bore barrel of his Red Ryder BB gun
Small boots trample urban forestry

He kneels in overgrown horseweed
to hide--hears a stutter of clinks and clanks
from the beak of a chirping song sparrow

He raises the barrel of his gun,
points it at the sandy gray russet
plumage perched above motionless
and dry-fires

The bird's bead eyes shoot
at him, so the boy cocks
his rifle, aims, then,
a crack and recoil

An explosion plumes from the bird's
white bosom. Its feet clutch in reflex—
body cascades back and
hangs there upside down

When the child grows older,
he will be ashamed to admit
he shot the bird once more
Not out of cruelty or grim fascination

Perhaps, pity

He couldn't stand to see it
dangling as useless and lifeless

as slung sneakers strung up
on a telephone line

After tossing his Christmas gift
into the garbage, he never
pointed a gun
at another living being

Grace

I remember being sat on the curb in front of her house.
I had walked to get there because my bike
had just been stolen by Sonia's brother.
I wasn't a hundred pounds yet, and
still so young that when I got upset
my eyes welled up with tears.

A voice from above me asked,
"What are you crying about, Javier?"
The heat of my cheeks stung my face on that cold night.
He asked, "Are the cuffs too tight, Guillermo?"

He ground the individually wrapped rose
I had just bought from 7-11 under his boot.
It only cost me 4 lunches and two breakfasts,
but it was meant for her and I could hear her
crying from her porch.

"Are you in a gang, Jorge? What you claim, ess-ay?"
I twisted my wrist in the nylon cable tie and made fists.
"Answer me, Ricardo! Alfonso! Jose!
Look at me, Julio! Enrique! Manuel!"

He tossed my 6th grade school ID onto my lap.
I ignored him as he drew his police baton
and smacked it into the palm of his hand.
I shook my head, not even slightly embarrassed by my photo,
I was going for the Michael Jackson look back then—
I just didn't understand why he didn't know my name.

As he raised the weapon over his head, he said,
"I'm going to ask you one more time, Ernesto,
Where are you from?"

Grace shouted from her front door,
Leave him alone! His name is Albert and
he's my friend!

He must have come to his senses
when their blue eyes met.
He cut me loose and drove away
in his black and white.

I'll never forget how her blonde hair
glowed beneath the porch light.

On My Way To See Colors

I'm on my pata mobile
heading south on Hawthorne
when two guys roll-up
in a dropped Chevy pick-up
hit me up—throw up
urban American sign language.
Pointer fingers touch tips of thumbs
like someone who has counted to three
or assuring you everything is okay.
But, it's not if you're a Blood.

8ecause, this soldier here
is a 8ritish Knight rep-ing hard.
8K—8lood Killer and he's so 6lue
he could 6e Grape St.
Jeri curl juice stains a dark cloud onto
navy 6lue upholstery.

I look up at the blue sky
and pray, then pan
from my heart to the gutter
to make sure
I am wearing the appropriate
                                  colors
for the occasion.

It's late in '88. Eazy-E blasts
through stolen Cerwins
from the Kenwood on the dash,
probably a Fosgate amp
and an Uzi on his lap.
I'm wearing my Angels hat

so when he starts to smile
I start to run.
But, before he started smiling,
he lifted up the gun.

Pissed
I was wearing my Payless sneakers,
I juke zigzags into blind spots
duck and dodge bullets
past a pristine white '74 Monte Carlo,

backseat looking like
someone took a sawed-off shotgun
to the cherry Kool-Aid man.
Before I hit the corner
I knew someone was dead—
Someone bleeding red or so true, blue.

When I got home
I asked my tío if I was a Blood or a Crip,
He said, *Tell 'em you're a democrat.*
Or, a republican. Better yet,
tell them you don't know.
Or, claim MOG.

I didn't know what any of it meant.
Later, I learned Democrats wear blue,
Republicans red, and MOG meant
My Own Gang.

I'm Going to Miss You, Dumbass

I can't believe you want me to feel sorry for you.
Isn't it bad enough
I had to wear a suit to your funeral?
I told you to wait for me but you didn't.
You popped onto the street like
a red light but the bus didn't stop.
You left me standing there
wondering how far the bus' tires
were going to take you traveling
in their treads.
I don't understand why
you always have to one-up me.
The whole world feels sorry for you
except for me
because your mom thinks it's my fault
we ditched school and sniffed spray paint
behind old man Johnson's hardware store.
She can't believe you thought you
were skinny enough
to lay under the bus
while it passed over you and
she feels bad that she didn't let you
eat more junk food.
What were you thinking?
Did you really think you were a superhero
like in one of your stupid comic books?
It was sniffing spray paint or
pissing on cars from the overpass like
we normally do, but you wanted to get high.
Our noses were glittering gold nuggets
turned up to a wavy sky.
Our eyes were red slits

like the cuts on our arms and everything was so funny.
I think I may have laughed
when one of your teeth
flew out of your mouth and
stuck into my cheek.
I'm going to keep it under my pillow.

Negro (Original Gangster)

Negro wasn't black, but
he was still a victim of society.
He was OG and
I remember how it used to be.
He was a woman's man--
no time to talk to his family.
He was always hustling.
Out there on the streets
making money
because the streets
were the only place
he could find a job.
He would come home after slanging and
tell me about gangbanging.
There wasn't a man
who could beat him down
but pigs would hold the bad wolf
to the ground and beat the brown off him.
He'd come home
spilling so much blood,
there were times you couldn't
recognize who he was.
In desperate times,
stealing and pawning gold rings.
Spending time in Sing Sing.
He'd write letters in beautiful ink
and remind me, "Mijo, have a dream."
He was just a victim of Justice,
given a life sentence the day he was born—
given a death sentence the day he was born.

The Last Time I See You
For Josephina

Her burnt behind flexes, then jiggles.
Legs skinny as Santa Monica Pier posts
perspire, take turns extending,
push the emaciated blonde bobbing her head
along the bike path north towards Venice Beach.
Waves crash hard. A child screams
in excitement and delight. The setting sun's
sides are stabbed by silver spear clouds.
An engine revs. A spare tire and jack clunk.
A trunk door squeaks as it closes overhead.
The world shakes, spins, wobbles, then
trembles as the camera spills out of your hand.
Your body follows with a thud—
teeth clack when chin hits pavement.
A car skids away, spitting dirt.
Sand showers you.
Then it reappears from out of the haze and
your bones crunch.
You are not crying.
Forward, reverse, forward, and you bleed
from your nose, your eyes, and ears;
face torn, clothes ripped.
A pachuca rushes out of her low-rider,
grabs the video camera,
fumbles with the buttons,
and then everything is black.

What You Won't Do For Love

I couldn't help but catcalling the fishnetted legs stepping through the industrial district in LA-- 7th street, just around the corner from Skid Row, we found big bosomed, big thighed, big lipped, big assed beauties looking for kids like us to buy their time, but we were so young . . . and I remember shouting profanities from the back of the pick-up truck, Show us what you got! Show us your . . . We just wanted them to show us anything we'd seen in bathroom stall magazines and we just wanted to know what women really looked like and we just wanted to have fun and the street stunk the salty and stale of dried cum and anal sex, but I didn't know it. The street smelled of desperation and despair but we didn't know it and we didn't know that only men had Adam's apples and we didn't know we should have been polite to women with Adam's apples. And, I thought the way to pick up on working women was to call them baby, and I didn't understand when one of them shouted back, Hey baby, your momma, hey baby! And we banged on the driver's side windows of men with their eyes rolled back getting blowjobs like we were playing ding-dong ditch on a boring Friday night and we didn't know why the black as ocean at night streets were filled with dried up squid. So, I can totally relate to how you are feeling. I can totally understand what you mean when you say you are tired of being alone.

Goodnight, Gorilla. Goodnight, Gangster

Now that I'm older, I have felt his pain. I've been broken, like him, a part of my mind missing. It hurts. It hurts, he repeats over and over. Until I hear grandpa say, "¡Ya! ¡No mas!" He enters the hall and kicks the bathroom door open easily. It swings open hard and hits my tío who is balled up on a pink ceramic tile floor. My tío Tony wails again. "Ow! Ow!" His voice is less whiny than it is desperate. In the streetlamp light coming through the bathroom window the blood is orange—the grout between the ceramic tiles on the sink counter is purple. There is blood sprayed across the shower curtain, the toilet lid, and the walls. It clings to the razor on the floor beside him. My grandpa yanks him up by his shirt in one swift motion and throws him into the garage-bedroom-sewing room-storage area. My grandma sleeps through the whole scene. I can hear my tío weep from where he is inside the garage. I want to help him but I just don't know how. The best thing I can think of is getting the Windex and cleaning up the blood he left behind. The last words I heard that night were my grandpa telling him, "Goddammit! Shut the hell up and go to bed! I have to get up early!"

A Tree Without Roots is Just Another Piece of Wood

1.
Here stands my grandpa,
Not Jose,
because these are the times when
white is right. So,
no way, Jose, but
Pvt. Joe Arzate. U.S. Army.
A proud veteran,
airborne wings tattooed on his log
of a leg to remind him
of the times he descended
into combat.

His eyes are black—
lost in the shadow of his
furrowed brows, or
the glare of summer sun.
It's '81.

Shirtless,
sweating,
rusty brown and chiseled
under thick black swirls of
hair grown too long and wild
over his ears.

His fists are boulders
wrapped in buffalo hide
clenched
like his teeth,
and he is snarling,

muttering,
"Never happen— never will",
in a tone that sounds like a dare.

2.
The Lakers are losing to the Celtics.
And, as if that is not enough to make
him sit forward in his recliner,
the music thumping through

the back of the neighbor's
candy apple red '64 Chevy Impala
is louder than announcer Chick Hearn.
It is more than my grandpa can tolerate.
So, after he slurps down a raw oyster
and a shot of tequila, he marches outside.

3.
Señora Sandoval
is on her hands and knees
scrubbing away sons.
I skip over the stream of
bleach, spilled blood, and tears
as it trickles down her driveway and
into the street.

A boy with his t-shirt stamped
Hecho En Mexico approaches
and suddenly his head seems
too heavy for him.
It falls to the side, and his hands rise,
fingers formed as though he is juggling invisible
avocadoes. Kingy, my grandpa's German Shepard
appears in front of me.
Kingy is taller than I am.

The kid stops, then
starts walking toward

his car. The back of his shirt says,
100% Mexican.

My grandfather takes
a step toward the boy
and says, "You better be going to
shut your trunk." And,
"If I have to come out here again…"
He growls,
"Never happen, never will!"

My grandpa points a finger
that seems as long as a Dodger dog and says,

"You better listen here.
I am an American.
I fought for the land
you snuck into, so
you better find the sense to treat
it and the ones
who fought to protect it
with respect."

4.
Now it's Dodgers vs the Pirates,
and the Pirates are winning
by a ridiculous amount.
When the game cuts to a commercial
my grandpa picks up the sports
page and studies draft stats.
I ask, "Grandpa,
If you're an American,
and he's a Mexican,
What am I?"
He licks him thumb,
turns a page, then replies,
"You are a Chicano, mijo." I tell him,
"But, my birth certificate says

I'm a Cauc-Asian?"
He chuckles,
"Never happened, never will, mijo.
Never happened, never will."

Fodder

Yesterday morning, the boy cupped corn dough grit in the soft of his small palm, sustaining golden brown, damp as that December morning, days away from Christmas Eve to be spent anxious for dawn, to wrap butter in thick flour tortillas, strip corn husks from meat filled masa, unwrap gifts he hopes are not made of cloth scraps grandma's sewn.

Grandpa was grey, cold, and sweat under homemade blankets. Oblivious of his grandson's kitchen contribution to the work of his wife and daughters, the Sports page trembled in his hands. A fly sat on the brim of his mug—crusted swatter at the edge of the table left unswung.

Last night the boy crept on linoleum floors glistening with the corpulent oily brown of infestation—listened to the jitter of the cucaracha at light switch. A bold few glared from countertops, wiry antennae flickered defiantly until their extermination echoed from greasy walls—the popping crunch under bedtime chanclas.

This morning, the boy examines something just as black and smooth in his tamale as his grandpa's eyes staring into what the boy cannot yet see, the smudge of ink on the discarded Times, and the empty chair beside him. The kitchen is quiet while he plucks last night's casualties from his breakfast.

Shag Carpet

Browns the variations of colors
of his family's skin
16 kids from 4 different women
wearing away the brown
shag carpet
beneath their feet
Brown panels of plastic wood walls
echo the snap of his brown leather belt
down the hall leading to his brown leather recliner
headrest stained by Tres Flores pomade and
he is sipping tequila under a blanket
my grandmother's hands made
watching the Lakers
hoping all he got paid
losing fingers while welding
doesn't get lost to his sports-pick gambling
The WWII veteran, The proud American
won't speak Spanish
to his 16 kids anymore
Doesn't speak to them much at all anymore
Locked up, knocked up, fucked up, cut down, shot down--
recovering from Lennox Park beat downs by Hawthorne Police
At least, on Sundays there is church and
time for God to bless America
and menudo--
fresh warm tortillas on the table--
enough food to share with the roaches
America's beer, Budweiser and
bud hung to dry by the water heater and
chili hot enough to make you grow hair
on your chest and make you
cry like a man

in one of grandma's novellas
and cars filled with enough gas to take on joy rides
and bent silver spoons for sons to cook heroin
Proud American
Apache first, but called a Mexican
Made children white on birth certificates
Proud American
Crayon Indian Red forgotten,
brown faded to grey
Proud American
Still just another dead American
buried on American soil
with a bottle of his favorite tequila
in brown panels of plastic wood
to be walked on by proud Americans

Conspiracy Theories

What hard working Chicana
wouldn't see the microwave oven
as a divinely inspired miraculous invention
to relieve the modern-day woman with 3 jobs
of her obligation to cook for 5 kids, 4 live-in grandchildren and
a traditional machismo viejo?

So, for about a week,
we became the scientific test subjects
of the physiological effects
of 10 cent frozen burritos
on the human body.

And, if it weren't for my extremely paranoid
tío Pancho and his conspiracy theories,
my grandma
would have never had to make another
meal on the stove.

I-z-pop-u-L-A-tion annia-L-A-tion.

Sabes, que? The CIA's selling the inner-city Crack.

Iz-pop-u-L-A-tion control.

Sabes, que? The AIDS epidemic
is chemical and biological warfare genocide.

It's population control.

Sabes, que?
I haven't seen any cacca-roaches in the kitchen
since you got that microwave . . .

If the cacca-roaches are laying low,
maybe it's time to let that thing go.
It's probably population control.

They want to take out Chicano's first.
Microwave burritos and Chimichangas.
Then, native American Indians with microwave popcorn.
The Italians are probably going to be next.
Just wait, there'll be microwave pizzas
in every freezer in LA.
I can't even watch the game
when that thing humming it's death song.
All the radiation messes up the reception.

IT'S POPULATION CONTROL!

Y, sabes, que, it was back
the aroma
of homemade tortillas
and Folger's coffee at 5 am,
waking to the sound
of my grumbling stomach,
papas frying in chorizo,
eggs sizzling in tablespoons of butter,
pink beans boiling
with a dash of salt,
a cube of pork,
onions and garlic
and my grandma
slamming the cabinets
to make sure she wasn't
the only one awake
before sunrise.

De Familia

He could have been one of my tíos,
Or even my father,
Wearing pleated black slacks,
A white tank-top,
Short haircut, thick mustache,
Polished shoes, and a silver chain
Draped from his leather belt
To his knees.
He leaned against a brand new
'57 Chevy Impala,
Head tilted back,
Challenging the capturer to—
Anything.
The photograph was old and
He had been Chicano for so long
The black and white
Aged a golden brown.

Birth to Death

1.
I am told that you were told by my father,
I was a girl.

I picture you dropping the avocado green
rotary dial receiver onto brown shag carpet.
Then, in your 1974 Ginger Glow Pinto,
running red lights through LA,
making street signs sway in your vortex.
I imagine your disappointment
when you were told my name is Fernando.
Although, I have no idea
what you might have wanted
to call me had I been a girl.
I wonder,
if before you saw my face for the first time
you had pictured the hundreds of dresses
you would have sewn for me.

2.
I went to see you at the hospital.
The shift nurse said you were sleeping.

The last time we spoke,
you told me you were tired.
I wanted to stand by your bed
and protect your sleep, but
the girl taking your vitals
was so nice, I knew
you would be safe with her.

3.
I went home, thought of the countless
tortillas you made for me, how many times
we had pastrami sandwiches together,
and of how disgusted you were
when served old coffee.
You had made it for over 70 years
and knew what it should taste like.
I remember the time you took scissors
to my Calla lilies.
I was furious.
You said, *It's because—
every once in a while,
we have to start over.*

I understand now.

4.
The last time you went to sleep,
I had just FaceTimed my dad.
He panned the room and
everyone in the family
was standing beside your bed—
except for me.
Your son's voice rasped like waves pulling away
from the shore through beach rocks.
He told me you did not have much longer.
Through a three-inch screen,
I saw you peacefully resting on your side,
I said, *Good night, grandma,* and
the beep of your heart monitor stopped.
One of your daughters collapsed onto you.
I smiled at my dad to comfort him,
but had no more words.

La Cocina

My abuelita wrapped my bones
in flour tortillas,
shaped my cheeks
from Manteca and
stained my blood
with chili that could put dark red hair
on a woman's chest.
She would bounce her dentures
off the table as I watched,
jaw dropped, spilling papas con chorizo
like drool, while she passed me
yesterday's news and tomorrow's coupons
to wipe my mouth.

I built castles in the grumbling refrigerator
from Tupperware filled with leftovers
that fed us through weeks when
16 hour workdays were not enough.

I could scratch the cracked eggshell walls
of her kitchen and smell the meals
cooked on the yellow gas stove
for three generations.

5 Fingers (Indica Leaf)

Red (dead-) head,
tanned, 21, shouts, Only $40!
Rasta string bikini breast triloquist beckons,
Are you ready? To get le-gaL!

Hemp green
scrub bottoms sag,
Sativa green g-string splits perfect portions.

Dirty blonde rootz girl spits peace.
Dreads sway tied up under a rainbow
Zig Zag bandana.

36C-26-36
Rucka tattooed—Day of the Dead
Calavera de azúcar - Vida La Vida,
takes my picture.

A rude girl rolls her red eyes
in response to an inquiry about
a certain Mr. Meanor
or whoever.
A lazy eyed MJ MD educates me on
Vitamin D, Fish oil, and Omega 3,
Government conspiracies and
the price of happiness,
then makes a recommendation.

I toke a dose of Venice Kush,
watch fool's gold set
in a smoggy hot pink sky.
Waves lap
wax Luna.

Long lines at Pizza by the Slice make sense.
Paranoid vendors burn people and
sweet cannabis scented incense
and I'm feeling irie.

Swapping Sillies

Happy-Faced-Clown puts it in Sad-Faced-Clown's hand.
Sad-Faced clown had never seen one before,
but she decides it is very realistic—
appreciates how the soft rubber feels like
genuine plucked chicken skin.
She notices it's considerable length, too.
It's much longer than she ever imagined.
When the sad-faced-clown squeezes it in her fist,
the rubber chicken squawks and she cannot contain herself.
She runs to the medicine cabinet and paints
a happy face over her sad face and laughs.

Now there are two Happy-Faced-Clowns.
They slip into love—
completely bananas
and skip the circus,
make a baby
and funny music
on top of the squawky
rubber chicken.

The very next morning,
Happy-Faced Clown runs off
with Firefighter Clown.
Happy-Faced-Pregnant Clown,
tosses the gag gift
into her bottomless waste basket.
It wheezes instead of squawks.
She paints a sad face on
before catching a ride
with Cab-Driver Clown
down to the abortion clinic.

Now she is back to her canvas tent
Sad-Faced Clown's pasty make-up
runs like mascara.
She takes the rubber chicken
from the trash and gives it a squeeze.
but it does not wheeze, squeak or squawk.
It simply lay lifeless in her fingerless cotton gloves.

Something She Was Going to Tell You

Part I: Going Anywhere

She is distracted by the way your eyes
flash a smile that could make
back-alley black streets wet.
It makes her sip sweat from her lip while
you talk too much about your tongue.
It works on other women, but she's different—
doesn't want you
inside, just feels safe with you beside her,
arms wrapped in yours
and you,
a straitjacket for this crazy town,
fit perfectly.

Tonight Buenaventura
is the bitter rambles
of a sweetly staggering
Sour Diesel smelling
      malignant madman
      moaning
berating—
boxing
past regrets
Unkempt nails
claw the swastika
stain stitched into his skin.
Boozed.
High,
wreaking
chaos.
Words like

punch drunk drool
spill into sidewalk
gutter.

He curses,
slurs-
screams.

Sirens
cry.
Women
wail.
Children
groan.
The common discord of a morning choir,
a collective bitter prayer to St. Bonaventure, but
the doctor is out and God has abandoned this place.

It's overwhelming—
Enough to make her hands moist.
She cups clouds in palms
or clutches sky,
mouth dry—
eddies a sigh.

She's back to you
and your baby blues—
the way they cradle
shadows cast from the random vagrant
wandering by, swaying below the Thelonious
that creeps through the crack of the window   up above-   on

Part II: The Second Story

Newlyweds
take cheap shots, but
miss each other
99 cents at a time.

Fling
plates and cups
fast and hard enough
to leave cuts and bruises.
Preferably scars.

Part III: Going Nowhere

You get thirsty,
take another swig while
she watches you dig
into the brim
of that 40. And,
she resists the impulse to
lick her lips—
send the wrong message.

It's raining,
plates and cups.
A baby bottle hits the pavement
and milk splatters in a pattern
that resembles warnings.
Wait. Not him. Not now.
Maybe, never.

THE MAN

County Zoo

The animals here in the zoo
are all guilty.
There are no innocents
doing push-ups to pass time,
staring at the ceiling doing sit-ups,
pacing cells,
peeking through cracks
for a glimpse of the world
outside our cages.
Our skin turns gray
as the floors, walls, bars, and justice.
We are provided public defender
pretenders and numbers
to replace our names—
the only thing we've ever truly owned.
We are stripped
of our dignity; Humbled—
given a shirt, pants, a pair of sandals,
a toothbrush, toothpaste, a comb,
a bed sheet, blanket,
and one roll of toilet paper.
(Our pillow gets smaller every time
we shit the shit they give us to eat.)
The clock on the wall taunts,
arms accusingly point at each of us
hacking away the seconds,
the minutes, the hours, the days.

Blind Faith

She's bronzed,
upright, blindfolded,
scales swing from her left hand.
She raises a double-edged sword.
Her armpits are shaved.

You exit the Ventura County Jail,
stop at the Lady Justice water fountain.
Spit clings to her cheek.
She's a sculpted erotic personification
of the morality of judicial systems.

Hunched forward
under the weight of the world,
her arms outstretched for balance.
Scales of justice sway
from pierced wrists.

Lips vandalized, spray-painted
a glossy blood-red smear,
legs bound in gold chains—
carnation pink toenails.
She wears US map cut out pasties.

Her breasts glow brilliantly.
She is propped by a sword
at her abdomen or
committing Seppuku.
The sun rises behind her.

You hear a zipper.
The basin of the fountain

glistens golden.
Toss in a good president
and make a wish.

Unnatural Remedies for Fairness

When I brought my son home from the hospital,
fresh from his mother's womb,
wrapped in a light blue blanket,
my grandmother cried, Pobre, Morenito.
She cupped her mouth with one hand,
ashamed for speaking Spanish,
then covered that hand with her other
in an involuntary motion to protect her
knuckles from the rap of a ruler—
the PTSD of surviving
a teacher with the privilege
of being born with light hair
and fair skin.
Pobre, Morenito, she cried.

She advised,
you must take a ripe tomato,
mash it into a cup,
then add a few drops of lemon juice.
Scrub the mixture into his skin regularly
or this world will never love him.

She would not hold my son.
As though his café skin,
richer than a dark roast Grande drip
was a plague that could be passed
through touch.
Pobre Morenito, she cried.

She advised,
Stir rose water into milk,
and mashed banana.

Rub this on his cheeks regularly
and he will get better grades in school.

Take milk powder,
papaya and honey.
Smear this on his forehead before bed
and by morning,
he will be invisible to the police.

Take egg white,
curd and oatmeal.
Apply it to his neck
and jobs will be handed to him.

Rub his arms with a skinned potato repeatedly
and no one will assume he speaks something
other than English.

A tiny amount of saffron mixed with olive oil
is the remedy for poverty.

Mix baking soda with water
and let it sit for 15 minutes.
Use it to bleach away his darkness and
no one will ever call him a…
Nevermind.
Such words will not be said in this house.

She never told me,
if I paint his skin,
he could be president one day.

Wonder Is Enough For Now

We watch the Sun sculpt
a waxing gibbous moon, and count
the pretty little accidents scattered
where brush strokes did not swipe pale indigo.

You observe the firmament—
Tell me, it looks close enough to touch.
I wait for you to say more;
knowing now is not yet time to tell you
we are always touching the sky,
flying through an expanding universe
in one dimension of multiple parallels,
because you are only 8. Just a boy.
And besides, what do I know?

For Fathers Who Pay to Have Their Children Beaten

My son is being taught self-defense.
I remember reading parents should not
rush to rescue their children
when they get hurt. He is crying and
not getting up from the mat, so
I wait and hope he is okay.

Now the professor is sitting beside my son
waiting for him to collect himself.
Even before seeing his teammate there
with his parents flanking either side of him,
I know which boy I paid to hurt my son again.
He reminds me of a kid I cannot forget.
The same unkempt shoulder length
greasy black hair, and the same
refried bean brown as me.

Rene, lay crumpled in the dry
grass and dirt, just outside
the chain link fence of our
elementary school.
I had resorted to my go-to move
so my enemy writhed
like a smothered worm and cried.
It was the only thing I had
ever been taught about fighting.

I don't recall what instigated her
to provide the simple solution to
all confrontations,
but my mother instructed,

"Whenever you get in a fight,
just kick him in the balls!"
This was the extent of my training.
I was so young I wondered what balls were.
The ancient technique worked
well enough for me to step away from Rene
who was busy cupping himself—
making mud puddles with his tears.
I bought a root beer popsicle
from the modified green van
drowning out the excitement
of the kids who gathered to spectate our brawl.

Circus music pumped from a speaker on its roof.

Before I could tear the clear plastic wrapper,
Rene jumped on my back trying to punch my ears
in wild haymaker swings. His fists
slapped against my forearms in loud clops.

When it was over again I bought another ice cream
and held it to my busted lip as I walked home.
I don't remember why we fought.

Shortly after that incident, my parents
decided I should learn to protect myself.
I was introduced to my Shotokan instructor,
a martial arts movie star,
who decorated the walls of the dojo
with very impressive pictures of himself
in flying kick poses.
At the end of every class
we were to line up and stand
with our legs wide apart
in a horse stance.
The sensei would kick us
in the balls three times
before class was dismissed.

Who is to say who is more hurt—
my son, one hand cupping his balls,
the other holding his throat?
Or, me, fighting back tears
when I reach him and see the pain
he is in. I ask him if he can breathe.
He nods. All I can do is advise
him to do what I have done
after being left on the floor,
aching in pain and crying—
one of the most important lessons
I learned when I was younger.
I tell him to, "Get up."

True Story

I am driving with my daughter and
there are these great clouds of the genus cumulus.
I tell her I can shape clouds with my mind.
Within minutes the cloud takes the form of a child's smiling face.
The image is so clear that my daughter is amazed by my gift.
Ironically, I believe she made the cloud change.
It looks just like her.

Bye, Dad

. . .he says. And, in my mind, I play the sound of his voice on repeat as though it's my favorite sad song. He's outgrown me, but he is slouched under his stuffed-full carry-on so we see eye to eye. Before he reaches the threshold of Gate A7, plane leaving for Dallas, warmth spills onto my cheeks like luggage tousled onto baggage claim trams.

16. Handsome. The flight stewards flirt with him. His cheeks blush, red as my eyes. I hope he hears me through his airpods and his long loose-curl purple hair under the hoodie he hides it with. I'm not sure if he hears me tell him I love him, and there may be time enough for me to tell him once more, but he turns his back to me and departs.

This is My Body

1.
He was cute. I mean,
blind eyes the blue of
the Blessed Virgin Mary's
mantle made the professor
noosed by scarlet velvet,
too pretty to call handsome.
He sat crowding the crotch
of his denim blue jeans, smiling.

I watched my wife dance
in her wedding gown;
The last woman I thought of before
placing myself in
the cups of his hands
to commune.

2.
The driver license
he handed me indicated
he was Javier James Tomas.
AGE: 37, EYES: Brown, HEIGHT: 6'3",
or incredible in bed
for a few more years— still a baby.
I'd stare down on him
down on me, looking up into me
wavering, eyes opening and closing
prayers for grace and mercy.
His height suggested his length and
I would have three different names
to moan while picturing whomever I wanted.

Example:
¡Ay, Javecito!
Oh, right there, Javier.
That's so good, James!
Así, Tomas!

Okay, make it four.

3.
After taking little sips off it,
he licked those thick lips of his wet,
set it on his tongue hard—
like he had something to prove.
I hope he remembers
how I stretched
and bruised his lips
every time he tastes
sacramental wine.

Antibiotic Antidepressants

Finish the bottle, that's what they always tell you. you never do because you feel better and want to keep a few around in case you start to feel sick again, but they are never there when you need them because every one of your house guests spend too much time in your bathroom double-flushing, spraying potpourri air-freshener, and lighting scented candles to hide the opening medicine cabinet creak and rattle of un-swallowed pills while they push aside

                                              children's vitamins bottles with unbroken seals and fumble with childproof bottle caps. They take one of every prescription they cannot pronounce and you let them because it is therapeutic—it makes you feel as though you are not the only one who is crazy and the voices in your head are really just the people trying to comfort you from your freshly painted white-walled bathroom while they search in your medicine cabinet for a way to be normal; a way to feel healthy.

Some search for love between stained sheets, while others search for death as though it's hidden between the sheets of their shredded wrists

I am forced to resist the temptation to tell you
that sometimes I kiss passed roach tips
more than I do my own kids lips.
I can't recall the last time
I placed my arms around the façade of my functioning family,
and when I realize this, I just hit it again and again and again
until the swerve of smoke spit reminds me
of my other woman's grinding hips.

She's the replacement
for an old habit—
a new addiction, a distraction,
a substitution, and
I'm not advocating prostitution, but
it cost a pretty penny to lure this lovely black girl
painted white face, playing the angel,
wearing a rubber-band armlet,
holding heaven in a drooling needle
to this place right here beside me
and she's too high to reach.
In the background, I hear Jim Morrison sing,
"I've been down so Goddamn long,
that it looks like up to me,"
and I know exactly what he means.

When the guilt wilts
my mind settles a bit.
I search for that next fix because

my woman isn't home,
but I can still hear her moans,
and the thought of tongue flicks,
like the slurping sounds in 69 flicks,
are starting to make me feel sick.
It makes me want to let my 9 spit
on the faces of those who leave traces
of semen on the breath of her sermons
when she preaches about her purity.
I'm so high
I'm afraid to move.
The strain might blowout my heart, if
I really have one.
I sit in front of this bullet proof glass black and white TV,
resting from the race which wore away my soul, if
I ever really had one, and I'm hoping
Mr. Reverend So-And-So
will have the time
to save a soul like me.
Can I get an amen?   No!
Amens aren't free. Salvation cost too much
money and I'm not buying it.
I've run away like another illegitimate prodigal son—
chased the white rabbit.
Now I carry his paw
in my back pocket,
but all it has brought me is bad luck.

There is a comfort here in his hole.
The light above hurts my eyes,
anyhow. I embrace the darkness,
press back against shadows until they climb into me
like lovers leaving tributes to themselves.
I search, but there are no red pills,
no blue pills, just empty bottles
which once contained
what could make me stop feeling.
Alice took them all and whispered before dead,

If life is but a dream,
death is an awakening . . .
She lost her head.
And now, everywhere,
there are Cheshire cats waiting to grin
so I am forced to resist the temptation
to tell you that sometimes times
the edge of a barrel
seems too far from the tip of the bullet.
My trigger-happy finger is too cowardly
to pull the cold metal comma between life
and death.

Finally Letting Go

My therapist
wanted me to tell you
I don't love you anymore.
I put your pictures in a box
with a pair of dirty socks to remind me
how much you stink.
I burned the letters you sent me.
Even the ones I wrote
and never sent to you.
The ashes are in the urn
above the fireplace where we hung
our stockings last Christmas.
I threw away
the pair of panties
I had stuffed in my pillowcase.
They stopped smelling like you and
they just don't fit me anymore.
I'm losing so much weight.
Every time I eat,
I think of you,
get sick and puke.
The bile is making my teeth rot, but
at least I can smile now because
I don't love you anymore.

She Spilled Out of Her Low Tide Blue Jeans

I watched her skinny dip
with a sunburned moon
It climbed above
the glistening funhouse vanity mirror
as languid sun set into clouds
stretching her visage
sending it rippling upon the ocean
like a flesh film
in a sleazy motel
on a black and white TV
with bad reception
      I was excited that
I caught a glimpse of a nipple,
even though
it was probably my own.

Dry Hump

Sitting on a sticky bus stop bench
in Los Angeles, there was a dog
humping my leg
The dumb bitch had no dick
Despite her persistence,
she wasn't enjoying herself,
so she tried licking my face

When do you become so alone
that a blonde
pit bull terrier
can make you shift in your chair
to hide your erection?

Insomnia:

It is only when we fail to dream that we are free to live

I take prescription dreams—
swallow enough sleeping pills
labeled Hope
to dream forever,
and I kiss my reflection passionately
in cold mirrors—
wet and sloppy,
slip in tongue for diversity,
write love notes to myself
in dank sighs
about my alter ego.

☺s and I ♥ YOUs fade

so I hesitate to label this substance abuse
or vanity.
It is a need to feel loved by someone,
anyone,
even if it means finding reasons
to love myself when
the person in the looking glass
is unfamiliar and incompatible.

1 Day in Perspective

2 cups of coffee
and a donut into the morning
or $5.05 o'clock and I was already
10 minutes late for work.
It was the double Windsor.
I should have used the 4-in-hand-knot.
2 junk mail deletes,
eleven good mornings
4 urgent replies, 3 CCs,
7 forced smiles and 1
undeliverable message brought
break time.
No new emails, a bottled water,
and a bowel movement meant cigarette break.
A stick of gum,
a voicemail and a callback before
my boss walks in.
Kiss ass until my lips are chapped.
Wipe nose.
Lunch time.
Chicken Curry, Miso soup,
and an unsweetened tea into my day,
or $2.00 tip o'clock and I was already
5 minutes late back from lunch.
I should have had the usual
4 Spicy Tuna Rolls and steamed rice.
"You need how many copies, of what?
I've got deadlines to meet! Per who?"
A paper jam-needs toner-warming up error,
400 black and white,
double-sided copies,
400 envelopes and 37¢ stamps

or $200.00 o'clock.
eleven goodbyes, 2 see-you-laters,
an onramp, a lane change,
a speeding ticket, an off ramp,
2 left turns and a parallel parking
until I was finally home.

Fluffy

she is wild,
uncontrollable and screams--
not for me
drying out
sweating in our living room
holding the flimsy green hose
seemingly capable of no more than a drool
as thick black creeps at me
so, I search with stinging eyes
the sun hides
in the blistering walls
heat plops in clumps from charred ceiling
trembles in puddles on the kitchen tile
the food stuffed cabinets cook
cans pop
windows shatter
the clatter of silverware
escaping the drawer
I ignore it all
as though none of this matters
I call for it in sore throat hisses
while curtains vanish like flash paper
and I can smell the hair on my arms
and the sofa, plastic, wood,
the wall mounted TV
and years of hoarded memories--
bitter
possessions singed
yet nothing is burning
except my lungs
everything is melting
a Dali painting on fire

family photo faces slide
from picture frames
to the floor
at her bedroom
I am reminded of the time
my dad told me not to pick up
the charcoal, it hurt
the time he told me not to sip
hot cocoa through a straw
I never listened . . .
besides, I can hear her sob,
hear her beg for me to save something
I can smell dead behind the door

Zombies Run 10ks

Tonight, open up your mouths and
let the world hear your pain.
Go ahead and cry—
Everyone is wearing their mask.

Tonight, boy blue
will let Roy G. Biv
rest on his tongue to
taste the rainbow.

Tonight roadkill
looks cool
smells like skunk kush.
Bats are welcome
to swing on my porch,
beautiful witches beg bluntly
toting hand stitched sacks.

Those naughty witches,
the ones you know by name,
spread their legs
to strap on broomsticks
and harvest spent seeds
with sweet street weed
cali-sage scented hair.
Girls in jack-o-lantern
candlelight.
Coy. Young again—
Gently stuffed with candy.

The Radical Pair Mechanism

Two quantum straphangers travel in opposite directions.
She's in a high-speed southbound Maglev that left Welloffville
4 years, 9 months and 16 days prior to his departure from
Nowherespecial.
He might as well have been on the slow train
edging along a common-er's rail from Misery Station.

Does it matter how long it will take for them to pass?
Their trains will collide without ever truly touching,
quite arguably the grandest illusion;
their brains' way of interpreting the interactions permeated in spacetime
between their electrons and electromagnetic fields.

It is their eyes that entangle them—
cryptochrome protein excited at the rear walls of their retinas.
Light intertwines with light
when they hallucinate each other into existence.
The Great Conductor would have them believe
Love is the great superconductor.
Zero resistance, the perfect state, but
chemical bonds will allow their electrons to latch-on to the imperfections
of one-another's skin creating the sensation of friction.

As their trains keep down their parallel tracks,
however far apart they are,
their fates remain woven.

Every Man's Fantasy
After Friday Gretchen, Every Woman's Fantasy

It could be the slap of the spank paddle
against her sigh soft creamy thigh
or snap of patent leather strip into
satin gloved palm.

The polka dotted kitchen window reflection
is insufficient, yet, I am lost in her—
A head cocked vampire watching
the sunrise on 8K Ultra HD TV
longing; aching to feel heat.

A pouty impatient dish-wash dominatrix
bathed in high efficiency LEDs
sits behind me
cross-legged in knee-highs
on a Bordeaux granite countertop
and makes me scrub
the metal off this fork.

You will have to wait,
cocina. You might
find me giving filthy detail
to disinfecting the bathroom
but only after I fluff these pillows,
stain release the seeded sheets,
iron those curtains,
separate thongs
from Gs, boyshorts
from briefs and breasts blessed bras,
there are yet spots
to be rubbed out

on the cream
tile floor.

Will you thank me
or spank me?

    Yeah—I hope so.

Far, But Not Gone

After drawing blinds
and dimming peach down lighting
she strikes a match
to light long wicks.
Smoke disseminates.
Leaves the scent
of cranberry and vanilla candles.
Flame licks space.
She flicks her wrist and tosses the stick,

yawns.
Covers her glossy lips
with the back of her hand.
One last draw of crisp air while
a siren's whine wanes
outside our window.
A cool breeze sighs
with the city's raspy hiss
through the dusty screen.
Her knees rise,
toes curl,
back arches as
she presses into organic cotton sheet—
Not a grind but a gyrating
back bone nudge.
She twists 300 thread count
into fists, wraps her legs
around the rope
as though to climb
into her dreams.
Her mouth spreads open,
eyes roll back,

lashes flutter,
chest expands and casts shadows
in the night gown valleys
of her rib cage canyons, falling to sleep,
cradled in our bed's arms.

Escape Velocity
for Neil Degrasse Tyson

One of my greatest fantasies has been to own a modifiable 2020 Blue Origin/Orion CST-100, Virgin Galactic Hybrid—escape sub-orbit borders, merge into low-earth altitude cumulus traffic, then challenge deep space listening to Prince's "If I was your girlfriend" on repeat while effervescent tears drift into zero gravity void from dwarf-star sore eyes. When the guttural throb of rocket thrusters settle and he screams plea-e-e-ease, his voice—bruised knees begging to be eased from concrete supplications of 9g drag-like loss. Hurling and aching as though from the indigestion of taking in countless swallowed balls of gas, hoping nebula trapped in lash curls and supermassive black hole pupils spaghettify every memory of you.

To Whom It May Concern

*For the girl who told me
I gave her the world
the day she was born.*

The nicotine stained fingernail moon
Scratched dark cold reason
Dug into the jagged silhouette
Of Mother's breast beneath
The milky sky

Believe me,
I suffocate myself
Place cigarette after cigarette
To my lips between gasps for air
And consume death
Time decays me As I age watching
Gaia, Venus, Mercury, Mars, Jupiter
And old Luna waltz amidst twinkling
Paparazzi flashbulbs
Mesmerized
A phenomenon
Of the anatomy
Of the human eye

In my mind's eye
I see you standing there
Gazing up at the same Gods,
And wonder, if instead,
They are gazing up at you

Watch Him Fall Forever

"If you are God's Son, jump. He will tell his angels to catch you in their arms. You will not hurt your feet on the stones below." – Luke 4:13

Graveyard, odd,
day, part-time,
night, moonlight,
hand, blow,
whack—
he'd have taken any job he could get and
she looked like a piece of work.
Legs longer than he had left in hours,
skirt shorter than he measured upright
in the crotch of his 33s—
she seemed young, new to the profession,
probably sucked fewer pricks
than she's smoked fags. She took a drag,
tore her nylons to keep 'em from looking snagged,
ratted her hair to keep it from getting messy and
smiled at him as she walked by.

This wasn't the chance in life
he had been waiting for, but
he would take what he could get.
He reached into his pocket, pressed
his back against the warm brick wall
of the abandoned church and prayed
to rub his copper against her silver skin.

When he looked up, she was gone.
So he staggered down the street
downing the only bottle of booze
he could buy with chump change, dragging

the lipstick tipped cigarette spit from her lips.
He pinched it between his teeth
as though it were one of her perky
nipples. Rolled over it,
stabbed at it, flicked
until the filter broke up and
his and her saliva flooded to the back of his throat.
He hacked—dark brown splat

against grey concrete. He
wiped the side of his mouth
with the back of his hand and
looked around to see who noticed.
No one did.
Everyone was in a hurry
going nowhere.

He rounded the corner quick—turning 40
if only he could sip more smog into his lungs but,
he's felt dead inside for years
so he scoped the 101,
watched cars from the overpass,
hoping this past sunrise was his last
and he searched for a place
to get to the end of his days—
to cut to the chase
'cause the cuts in his arms
didn't do the job.
Maybe if he could have found one
he'd still have his kids,
his car, his house, his dog and his old lady, too.
Jumping seemed like the only thing left to do.

Zero Tolerance: Miseducation
after Federico García Lorca, New York (Office and Denunciation)

Beneath laws sprawled out on jaundiced pages
like Rorschach inkblots,
division,
two individual drops of blood divided by a wall,
standardized tests of humanity
answer sheet bubbles
remain empty choices
Their whole life, endless empty choices
leading past high rise city suites,
sundecked dog mansions,
the aroma of fresh baked
gourmet pet treats--paths leading
to corporate kennel cages
where Las Lloronas wail
on the other side of a wall
that only the blind still want to build.
Deportation's orphans know the wall
already exists.
Without the luxury of wearing priceless
white privilege glasses, too.
But, these tender age children,
the orchestra conducted by foot soldiers
did not come to see this border--
to see the people of the sun
cast shadows on concrete floors--
they are all that's left behind.
Between whiteboard residue removed
with EverWhite sheets, watch color bleed
bleached back past invisible lines.
Lives emptied.
Realities pummeled,

left gash red, bruised blue
and seeing stars.
Pledging hands once held over hearts--
empty.
Every day at the border, they slaughter,
11 million people,
8 million workers,
20 thousand children to accommodate heartless
ICE cold employment,
7 million "bad hombres,"
1 million mothers--
forever disembodied families.

The orphans and laborers,
and the "drug dealers, rapists"--
the "bad hombres", and mothers,
the "animals" lay their heads between
division and subtraction symbols where
zero tolerance equals zero humanity,
terrified by the wailing Lloronas.
It's better for Dreamers to keep dreaming
while nightmares fill dawns with distress or
anxiety disorders rather than to resist
the endless wailing,
the endless bleaching of color,
and the purging of hope, shackled
by pale patriotics.

I denounce all those
big lie believers
who never think of anyone
other than themselves,
who add bricks to the wall
that's already been built,
"where the hearts of little
forgotten animals beat"
against cages--
where the test of humanity is failed.

I spit tears in your faces.

The rest of you are me.
Stirred and restless,
revulsed by capitalists' greed,
whose smiles drool the blood
of exploited, masticated lives.
This county is heaven
that is not yet yours
and ruled by demons.
This is paradise lost.
There are flags made of natural fiber
being snagged, thread by thread
and I hear the meta parody anthem
sung by a choir of megalomaniacal narcissists
with notes that shatter glass ceilings.
I am only a desperate whisper.
What more can I do than ask the ICE to melt
one warm breath at a time?

Or, return hearts to hands that once pledged
allegiance to national ethos?
While I kneel, you may step upon my back
to climb back over to heaven which rejects you.

Floating Echo

There are so many waves for knee boarders
to kneel upon and worship at my salty bloated feet
but I wean from shore,
from the muttering women thumbing beads
and men wearing crucifix nooses,
And the, and the…
OHM.

This morning, as every other morning
I find myself
Enlightened
    by dawn
        nourished by the breath of men
long since dead.
Rain thuds upon my breast giving me
a heartbeat quiet as the crackle of
a single grain of dry rice
chewed by a monk with dentures.

Transmigrating over distilled blue
Upon this lotus leaf raft
Subjectively existing
A shell of self
Transpicuous rubbernecking
Buoyant flotsam
Yellow duckies, green frogs, blue turtles and red beavers
and the, and the…

…OHM

Manufactured
plastic

reflections
Coexisting
man-made nature
animals, beings
in the serene peace of ocean sway

The Walking Dead

This boy's hair is black as oil spilled
on rainbow sheen plastic
polluted ocean's
water fowl wings.
He holds a fistful of fracking flow-back
contaminated dirt—
the color of his mother's stinging hazel eyes,
knees grass stained green,
legs scratched Round-Up rash
sulfuric acid aerosol sunset-sky-red.

He shakes his head.
His loving mother's almost dead.

His snakeskin dry arms itch
as he waves
           hi
to the skanking meth-head tweaking on
radiated asphalt
      with the slight seismic twitch
of a psychotropic substance smile.

She reminds him
of his sister's methylated spirit
stillborn from wellbores injected
before all those broke folk
went blind and took toxin
deep sleep comatose naps.

An old metal Mustang coughs
grey into bronchitis brown smog
past the asthmatic young faces of his hungry friends,

obscuring elbows propped in tinted windows
of houses with eviction notices taped
to wrought iron screen doors
under cement milk carton rooftops.

Mother, nature is almost dead.
Mother, earth is almost dead.
At least, that's what his uncle Sam said.
The tree of life in his desolate garden decays
Bark crumbles to dust
Fruit rots
Macroorganism hollow roots

and the fun guy exploits
its fallen branches.

The thought warms his mindful globe.

He shakes his head
and wishes it weren't true, but
you can't make wishes on the chemtrails
of planes roaring overhead.
Oh, big brother, what is he to do?
You can't make wishes on
artificial shooting stars
droning through the sky.
Nothing left for him to do, but hang
his head and cry. Just sit
and watch the walking dead go by.

M249 Squad Automatic Weapon

With his camera—
the light-machine gun,
14.4 pounds lighter than the SAW,
he shoots from various positions
in challenging environments
without fatigue—
with accuracy and ease.
He wants to capture death now
rather than cause it.

We talk about conspiracy.

The classroom smells like a men's locker room
after a football game that went into overtime.
The student tells me,
"Nothing feels as good as war—
not even sex."
I cannot relate to him.

He says, "A photographer
once retouched a slice of pepperoni pizza
until it resembled a supermodel."
I reply, "He must have been pretty lonely."
Then, the student shows me a woman
with flawless skin.
He had laboriously blurred each pore of her face.
I mumble some cliché,
"I guess you can't believe everything you see."

He asks, "What is left to believe in?"

Resilience

See, I'm THAT cholo.
The weight of my 9 got my pants saggin,
I keep 'em crimped and baggy.
I ride low on drive bys
so I can I watch the bullets fly
while neighbors dive
into pools of ancestral blood.

This is how we survive.
This is what resilience looks like . . .

C me?
I'm that OG
straight out the penitentiary.
The place they made me spread my cheeks
to let that hura take a peak--
where I learned to keep
my soap on a rope
'cause I sold dope trying to cope
with racialized unemployment.
See?

I'm the MECHA member
in the immaculate conception shelter
wrestling life's dreams on a bottom bunk,
listening to the man above
murmur about dying.
And, that's my mother crying--
She, the movement in the distance.
Her resistance wasn't enough
to keep them from raping her--
but at least we got a roof over our heads
and we're fed.

This is resilience.

Teacher wants me
to write about my feelings?
You know what it feels like
to be stabbed 3 times?
Resilience looks like me
trying to get this GED,
or the loca stabbed 20 times
4 months after being shot
taking pops at cops after
bong rips and whiskey sips—
Don't trip . . .

over the abuela scrubbing blood
off curbs with her tears and snot
'cause these clika's streets are hot.
She can show where
lopped heads feed flowers
buried in the barrio botanical garden
but not until after Sunday
confessions to pedophiles
keeping seedier secret than hers.

It's the kid still graduating college after
his uncle got out of prison –
you remember that OG?
He taught his educated nephew
pillows taste like pain
but leave you feeling emptier than that
vato pushing a ¼ lb
of inexpensive death
wrapped in pretty color paper
toward you
The stuff is killing you,
but the jobs feed him
and his family--
keep his probation officer happy, too.

Resilience.

It is reconstructive surgery
after pig hooves concuss you
into concrete cracks
without repercussion
or convictions, see . . .
Resilience ain't pretty—
ain't something you want
looking back at you in the mirror.

Can you hear it?
Me praying--Dear God, this is my body.
Do you even remember me?
I look like closed caskets
for childhood friends and
bruised knees behind pews
praying You will forgive me
for selling myself from corner markets
slanging lips on cocks
clocking glocks for ready-rocks
in clumsy English
cause Spanish is frowned upon . . .

Listen, I didn't have to sell out to be sold
from my classroom to his private prison slave plantations.
We used to call them chains, but
now we call them cuffs and we've all worn them.
Enslavement feels a lot like resilience.

This is my blood
I'm testing positive--
Spilling like Old E
from 40s for lost homies.
I'm the girl getting pushed around
the ward in a wheelchair
'cause I'm trying to kick meth
but I can't move my legs--

can't wait to get back to the boy
with the sticky that makes my eyes roll back
like a thousand orgasms
after one needle prick.
I'm that meth head walking dead
smiling cause I still have a few teeth left
'cause I'm so resilient.

Yeah, this is resilience.
It almost kills us.
But, we got this.
You've got this.
You got it?

No!

I will not calm down!
You have a gun pointed at his chest
telling me he's under arrest—arrest?!
Because he supposedly ran a stop sign?
Why didn't you pull us over at the time?

Look!
We are at our home,
standing in our own yard.
His hands are up,
His back is turned to you now . . .
They won't let people kneel in protest but
you want him to get on his knees?
Please.
He is not a slave.

Why are you doing this?
Why is there 10 of you here for one man?!
Why is there more of you coming?
For a stop sign?!
Don't you have anything better to do
with your time?
You wouldn't even come into this neighborhood
when my house got broken into.

And, you!
You ought to be ashamed of yourself!
Wearing that badge while you stand there
watching those men kick the color of YOUR
skin on my boy's face.
He's not fighting back.
His hands are cuffed behind his back.

You're hurting him!
He's my son. If things don't change
he could be your son, too, one day!
So, no! I will not calm down!

What do you need that K9 for?
How is he supposed to relax?
There are 20 of you
and only one of him and
he hasn't done anything wrong!

This isn't right! Dear God,
why couldn't you make us . . .

I swear I saw you at that kkk rally
the other night!

Okay. Okay . . .
No, this is not okay.
I'm searching for peace in my life.
I will not tolerate hate,
but you peace officers love
killing people like us!
And, I'm starting to hate people like you.
It's not okay for you to treat people
the way you do--
So, no, I will not calm down!

Why are all of you here?!—
To watch my boy get his head
slammed into the dirt?
You tore his shirt!
I just got that for him
when he graduated college.
They don't teach this kind of knowledge—
How to defend yourself from men who hate the color of your skin . . .
They told him his education
would protect him

but you devils was lying again.

No, I will not calm down!
You got cop cars lined up deep
on my block—
painted black like you knew you were coming to my son's funeral.
You aren't here to protect anybody!
You profile, detain and kill
if you can get away with it.
And, all I can do is stand here and
run this camera?

No, I will not calm down.
We're already scared of you.
What are you trying to prove?

He ain't even conscious.
Please! Somebody stop this!

What did he do?
What did he do?

Why are you doing this to him?
Why are you doing this to us?
Why?

For a stop sign?

Orange Man Versus the Universe
for Gil Scott-Heron

We got a Space Force to protect us now from
little green men on the moon.
We can't get ourselves up there, but
they ain't coming here
no time soon.
Orange man
don't want no little green men
immigrating from the moon. So,
we got a Space Force to protect us from
little green men on the moon.

He don't want no healthcare for all
He don't want you to breathe clean air at all
He don't want those dreamers dreaming
and he sure don't want no women leading

But we got ourselves
a Space Force to protect us from
little green men on the moon.
We can't build no walls up there, but
they ain't coming here
no time soon.

Most can't buy their way into college
can't afford that higher knowledge
30 years from now I'll be paying still
Unemployed, broke, and feeling ill

But we got ourselves a Space Force
to protect us from
little green men on the moon.

Cost too much to put cages there, but
they ain't coming here
no time soon.

And what we eat is causing Cancer
Orange man says he might have the answer
How my supposed to believe what I hear
Little man, my dad died last year
Orange man go round collected taxes
Spends time on the golf course, relaxes
Got himself a pretty wife, but
she didn't sleep with him last night—
Can't seem to tell the truth,
Spits on people from the Trump Tower roof
Orange man running out of alibis
Saying it's everyone else who lies
Please do something more than Tweet
127,000 times last week?
Don't you know you could be taking action
Instead of typing up all them distractions

We got a Space Force to protect us now from
little green men on the moon.
We can't get ourselves up there, but
they ain't coming here
no time soon.
Orange man
don't want no little green men
immigrating from the moon. So,
we got a Space Force to protect us now from
little green men on the moon.

Let's Go
after Walt Whitman's, Song of the Open Road

You used to give Him strength
when you still believed in Him.
I said, When you still believed in Him,
You used to give Him strength
                                    so,
stop bitching to me about God.

Maybe He was tired.
Have you ever worn so many hats
you inspired Dr. Zeus Seuss? Zoot Suits
24/6 straight in a 7-day week?
Have you ever been a Carpenter/
Gardener/Artist/Architect/Educator
who spoke in parables like a poet—
breathed words into ghost writers' minds . . .

etcetera, etcetera. Morrissey sings,
"In the midst of life
we are in death . . ."   Excedrin.

I bet he'd rather crack open a bottle of beer
waking up—baking up
companies like Cinn-a-sinny-bonbon
in the oven of His mind,
smoke a J of His Earth's harvest
Moon full
rests her head against Dawn's
warm pillow.
Maybe He wanted to slam
the cosmic snooze button,
take a shower

after making Love
to Venus before getting out of
the universal Tempur-Pedic bed.
The time is now, He thought.
Get up. The time is now. I won't do it alone.
I know I'm not alone. Let's go!

Jesus could have teleported but, He walked.
His legs are strong.
His lungs are strong.
His arms are strong.
His shoulders prepared
to take creation from the void and
place it onto His back again.

Jesus is probably really pronounced
Hey, Zeus, the living water,
a true wetback—
brown because He is not afraid
to play in the sun, back wet because
He is not afraid
to work in the sun.

Wetback got smart.
Wetback got a drivers permit. Wetback got a job.
Wetback is someone's daughter—
someone's son.
                                        Just like you.

We are forced to bear the darkness
the scars of our kinfolk
kick shackles to jazz beats
spit spliff smoke
pump fists for freedom.

America, we are slaves because we choose to be.

Get off your knees.

Stop praying—begging Him
to come in for overtime
on His day off.
Get up! Do something!
He's only one man.
He can only feed
so many people alone.
Let's go!
He can only solve
so many problems alone.

Let's go!

Biography

Born in Los Angeles County, Fox Hills, California, Fernando Albert Salinas received a Master of Fine Arts in Creative Writing with an emphasis in Entertainment from Full Sail University and a Bachelor of Arts in English at California State University, Channel Islands. He is on the Board of Directors, the Ventura County Area Coordinator, and a Master Poet-Teacher for California Poets in the Schools. He is also an Adjunct Professor of English at Ventura College, the Ventura County Area Coordinator and recitation coach for the California Arts Council's Poetry Out Loud program, and the Editor-in-chief for Spit Shine Publishing. As Literary Arts Program Coordinator for the Ventura County Arts Council, he focuses on enhancing the presence and appreciation of poetry and the literary arts, raising awareness of the power of literature, poetry, and the spoken word. In 2012, Salinas initiated the Groundswell Committee: a small collection of local poets, with the support of the Ventura County Arts Council, and created the County's poet laureate program. In 2018, he implemented a youth poet laureate program for the county. His book, *The Misadventures of the Barrio Boys of Guadalupe*, was published in September, 2021. He has performed his spoken word internationally.

For more about Fernando Albert Salinas, visit: FernandoAlbertSalinas.com

www.ingramcontent.com/pod-product-compliance
Lightning Source LLC
Chambersburg PA
CBHW011405070526
44577CB00004B/409